61690

W9-AUY-117

The North American Bison

Other titles in the Returning Wildlife series include:

The Bald Eagle
Bats
Manatees
The North American Beaver
North American River Otters
Wild Turkeys

Special Thanks To:

Trudy Ecoffey, Oglala Lakota College
Cindy Hoffman, U.S. Fish and Wildlife Service
Pat Jamieson, U.S. Fish and Wildlife Service
Steven Johnson, Bronx Zoo
Don Lake, InterTribal Bison Cooperative
Lori Monska, Columbus Zoo and Aquarium
Dr. Harold Picton
Misty Smith, Wild Winds National Buffalo Preserve
Dr. Al Steuter, Nature Conservancy
Dr. John Trippy, Wild Winds National Buffalo Preserve
Amy Wright, National Wildlife Federation

Returning Wildlife

The North American Bison

John E. Becker

KIDHAVEN
PRESS™

THOMSON

GALE

San Diego • Detroit • New York • San Francisco • Cleveland
New Haven, Conn. • Waterville, Maine • London • Munich

THOMSON

✦

™

GALE

To Aunt Jane, who has been such a wonderful influence in my life.

© 2003 by KidHaven Press. KidHaven Press is an imprint of The Gale Group, Inc., a division of Thomson Learning, Inc.

KidHaven™ and Thomson Learning™ are trademarks used herein under license.

For more information, contact
KidHaven Press
27500 Drake Rd.
Farmington Hills, MI 48331-3535
Or you can visit our Internet site at http://www.gale.com

LIBRARY OF CONGRESS CATALOGING-IN-PUBLICATION DATA

Becker, John E., 1942–
    The North American bison / by John E. Becker.
       p. cm. — (Returning wildlife)
Summary: Describes the physical characteristics, behavior, habitat, life cycle, and endangered status of the North American bison.
Includes bibliographical references and index.
    ISBN 0-7377-1380-1 (hardback : alk. paper)
    1. American bison—North America—Juvenile literature. 2. Endangered species—North America—Juvenile literature. 3. Wildlife conservation—North America—Juvenile literature. [1. Bison. 2. Endangered species.] I. Title. II. Series.
    QL737.U53 B46 2003
    599.64'3—dc21
                                                2002003809

Printed in the United States of America

Contents

chapter 1

North American Giant

When Europeans first arrived in the New World, more than 30 million bison roamed North America. By the late 1800s the huge herds of bison had been hunted almost to extinction. At that time, the few remaining bison lived in national parks, zoos, or private herds.

Early in the twentieth century the **American Bison Society** was founded with the goal of saving the species. Through their efforts, and with the help of other organizations, government agencies, and private individuals, bison numbers gradually increased over the years. Today, bison have recovered, and they number more than 350,000.

Survivor of the Age of Giants

Bison have lived on Earth for more than 2 million years. They first appeared in Asia and Europe before crossing the land bridge connecting Asia and North America during a time when much of the Northern Hemisphere was covered with ice—approximately 250,000 years ago. The ancient bison of that period were much larger than today's bison. They weighed as much as five thousand pounds (more than twice the size of modern bison) with horns up to eleven feet across.

Giant bison lived in North America with other gigantic mammals such as wooly mammoths, mastodons, giant beavers, and saber-toothed cats. Sometime after humans came into North America from Asia—approximately twenty thousand years ago, most of those large mammals, including the giant bison, died out. Smaller bison managed

The North American bison roamed the earth for over 2 million years, before European settlers hunted them almost to extinction.

to survive, however, and flourished across North America. At one time, bison could be found from Alaska, throughout Canada, the United States, Mexico, and into Central America.

Today, there are two subspecies of North American bison, the plains bison (*Bison bison bison*) and the wood bison (*Bison bison athabascae*). They are related to the European bison or wisent (*Bison bonasus*). When early

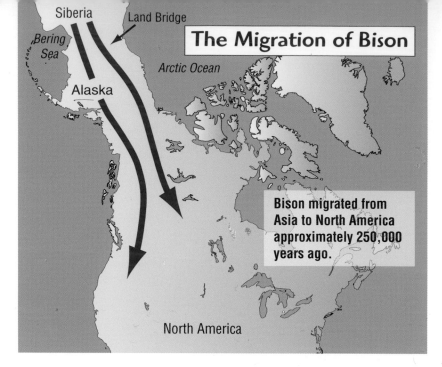

The Migration of Bison

Siberia
Land Bridge
Bering Sea
Arctic Ocean
Alaska

Bison migrated from Asia to North America approximately 250,000 years ago.

North America

European settlers first saw North American bison, they mistakenly thought they were a type of buffalo and called them by that name. True buffalos include the water buffalo of Asia and the Cape buffalo of Africa. There are no true buffalos in North America.

Prairie King

About 12,500 years ago, when the last glaciers that covered North America melted, they left behind a large area of grasslands that covered the middle third of the continent. Those grasslands, known as the Great Plains, extended from the Canadian forests in the North, to the Gulf of Mexico in the South, and from the Rocky Mountains in the West, almost to the Mississippi River in the East. Without vast areas of grasslands, bison could not have grown into the enormous herds that pioneers found on the Great Plains early in the nineteenth century.

Early French explorers used the French word for grasslands—**prairie**, and that name is still used today. Prairies provide ideal habitat for **grazing** animals such as bison. Bison have teeth that are made for grinding plants

North American bison (bottom) are sometimes mistaken for buffalo.
Buffalo (top) only live in Asia and Africa.

such as grass, and they have stomachs that absorb the nutrients found in grass. Everything a bison needs for survival can be found on the prairie.

Bison, in return, help the grasslands to continue growing. When bison eat, they chew off the tender tops of the grass but leave the base and roots to grow again. As they pass through an area, bison leave behind their droppings, which fertilize the grass, allowing it to grow strong. One hearty type of grass that bison prefer to eat is buffalo grass. It is a nutritious grass that grows near buffalo wallows (where bison roll in the dirt and mud to remove biting insects) after the bison have moved on. Bison also help grass to spread to new areas when the grass seeds stick to their coats.

Native Americans who lived on the Great Plains depended on the bison. Those tribes followed the bison as they roamed across the prairies searching for fresh grass to eat. The Indians killed just enough bison to obtain the food, clothing, shelter, and weapons they needed to survive. Native Americans used every part of the bison and thanked the Great Spirit for the gifts they received from their bison "brothers."

Thunder Across the Plains

Bison are some of the largest mammals found in North America. Adult male bison, called bulls, can stand six feet tall at the shoulder and weigh two thousand pounds. Females, called cows, stand about five feet tall at the shoulder and weigh more than seven hundred pounds. Both males and females have heavy, curved horns.

North American bison are easily recognized because of a large hump at the shoulder (larger in males than in females) and thick hair around the head, neck, and shoulder. Bison are usually dark brown in color, but on rare occasions one may be white.

A bison rolls in the dusty grass to scratch its back and remove tiny biting insects.

When bison calves are born in April or May, nine to nine and a half months after the fall breeding season, they are reddish brown in color. The calves are large at birth, weighing up to fifty pounds. Cows generally give birth to a single calf each year, but occasionally a cow may have twins. Because of the threat of predators, calves are usually up and running within three hours of being born.

A few weeks after birth, calves turn brown and then almost black like the adults. Calves are almost full grown by their fourth year, but they will continue growing for another two or three years. Wild bison generally live from fifteen to twenty-five years, and a female may continue breeding for most of her life.

While grazing on buffalo grass, a bison calf stops for a sip of mother's milk.

Like other animals, bison communicate with each other through sounds. Most often cows "talk" to their calves by making a muttering, grunting sound. The calves answer with a similar sound.

Bison are social animals that live together in herds. A herd is made up of cows, their offspring, and a number of young bulls. The herd provides protection from predators. When the herd is grazing, calves are kept in the center of the feeding area as alert cows keep watch. Bison rely more on their excellent sense of hearing or smell, however, because their eyesight is not well developed.

Bison herds once numbered in the hundreds of thousands. Early settlers on the Great Plains reported seeing herds of bison that stretched as far as the eye could see and made a sound like thunder when they ran. Usually, bison walk slowly or trot, but a bison can run up to thirty-five miles per hour.

Bison Predators

Wolves and grizzly bears are the only predators to pose a serious threat to bison. When huge herds of bison covered the Great Plains, more than 1 million wolves may have followed the herds. Normally, a pack of wolves will not attack a healthy, full-grown bison. But young, injured, or sick bison are easy prey. In winter, wolves will attack the last member of a herd as the bison walk single file through deep snow.

Wolves are one of two primary predators of bison.

Because of their size, strength, and fearlessness, grizzly bears are also a threat to bison. A grizzly bear will even attack young bulls if they are separated from the herd, but the bear risks injury or death if it attacks an adult bull. Most often, however, grizzly bears eat bison when they drive wolves away from the carcass of a bison that the wolves have killed.

While predators took a number of bison, they were never a threat to the survival of the species. Overhunting by humans, however, is what almost drove bison to extinction.

chapter 2

Slaughter on the Prairies

Bison are easy targets for hunters because of their great size and habit of living in large herds. For centuries Native Americans, on foot and armed with only spears or bows and arrows, hunted bison. But when whites began hunting bison using guns and riding horseback, bison populations declined rapidly.

Decline

As Europeans settled in North America, they found bison scattered along the Atlantic coast from Virginia to Georgia. Bison had not lived in that region for very long before the

Native Americans hunted bison with bows and arrows or spears.

colonists arrived, however. From stories of early settlers, it appears that the bison had made their way into western Pennsylvania, Virginia, the Carolinas, Georgia, Tennessee, Kentucky, and West Virginia from Ohio. Between Ohio and the Mississippi River, herds were living in Indiana, Illinois, and Wisconsin.

Because other animals were so plentiful, the settlers did not consider bison an important source of food. The settlers still shot them, however, and by 1770 bison were gone from Georgia.

Herds as large as three hundred were reported in South Carolina, but bison were also gone from that region by 1775. In Tennessee and Kentucky, herds as large as fifteen hundred were seen, but by the early 1800s bison had disappeared from those regions, as well as all the territory east of the Mississippi River.

By the middle of the nineteenth century many bison were killed by settlers crossing the Great Plains over the Oregon Trail and other trails to the West. Hunters also saw an opportunity to cash in on the travelers' need for meat by killing bison and selling the meat to wagon trains.

Coming of the Railroad

In 1863 work began on the Transcontinental Railway to connect the eastern United States with the Pacific coast. The Union Pacific Railroad began laying track from the East at Omaha, Nebraska, and the Central Pacific Railroad began laying track from Sacramento, California, in the West.

At the height of construction, each railroad employed nearly ten thousand workers. To feed those workers, the railroads hired professional hunters. Because bison were plentiful on the plains, the hunters had no trouble killing them for food. The hunters also shot many more bison for "sport," leaving the dead bison where they fell.

One famous hunter who shot bison to feed railroad workers was William F. "Buffalo Bill" Cody. Cody claimed to have killed more than forty-two hundred bison in an eighteen-month period. He was only one of many hunters who boasted of killing great numbers of bison. By the time the Transcontinental Railway was completed in 1869, many thousands of bison had been killed.

At that same time, many former Civil War soldiers went to the Great Plains to make a living by hunting bison. The railroads made it easy to transport bison products to markets in the East and "hide hunters," as they were known, shipped tons of bison skins by rail. Tanners in Europe and America discovered ways to make a variety of products from bison hides such as shoes, belts for

A poster advertises the arrival of William F. Cody, better known as Buffalo Bill. He boasted of killing thousands of bison.

COL. W. F. CODY

I AM COMING

machines, and clothing. As new uses were found for bison products, the demand steadily increased. The price of bison hides varied considerably, but even at $1.25 per hide, hide hunters made a good profit by killing thousands of bison each year.

Hunters also killed bison for their meat. Bison meat, especially the tongue, became a popular item in restaurants during that time. Many hunters were hired to kill bison to meet the growing demand. This practice, called market hunting, caused bison to be slaughtered in even greater numbers.

Some hunters were also hired by the railroads to shoot bison that caused long delays as the trains waited for the bison to slowly cross the tracks. Before long, passengers were also joining in the "fun," and many bison were killed by passengers shooting from the windows or platforms of moving trains. As a way to get people to ride the trains, railroads advertised that passengers could pay $10 for a round-trip ticket to shoot bison. Shooting bison was referred to as "plinking," and travelers considered the plinking of bison a great "sport."

Wealthy people from other countries came to America to experience the "thrill of hunting buffalo" on the Great Plains. Bison hunts were compared to hunting wild animals in Africa, even though the bison were as easily shot as cattle standing in a corral. One of the more well-known buffalo hunters was Grand Duke Alexis of Russia, who celebrated his birthday with a "buffalo safari" in which he and his friends killed ninety bison in two days. That paled by comparison, however, with Sir Saint George Gore of Ireland, who killed more than two thousand bison.

Casualty of War

When the number of whites in Indian Territory continued to increase, full-scale warfare broke out. To protect their

Bison tongue was considered a delicacy in the nineteenth century.

way of life, Indians attacked the whites and the U.S. government sent federal troops into the area to protect its citizens. In the 1870s the situation was so serious that the government sent an army to the plains to deal with the "Indian Problem."

One casualty of these wars was the bison. The growing number of American troops in the area needed to be

19

A bison carcass rots in the snow after being slaughtered by soldiers.

fed, and bison were easy to kill. The soldiers shot the bison they needed to eat, and more.

Also in the 1870s, gold was discovered in the Black Hills of the Dakota Territory. The shiny metal was worthless to the Sioux Nation, who considered the Black Hills their sacred land. But when news of the gold discovery reached the rest of the country, fortune seekers flooded into the Dakotas. Although the Sioux killed many of the prospectors, they kept coming.

President Ulysses S. Grant understood that the Indians legally owned the Black Hills. But when an attempt to buy the territory from the Sioux failed, President Grant decided to use military force to drive the Sioux onto **reservations** and open the area to gold miners. Thereafter, several major battles were fought, including the famous Battle of the Little Bighorn, in which Lieutenant Colonel George A. Custer and his soldiers were killed.

President Ulysses S. Grant (pictured) ordered Native Americans onto reservations.

As the conflict continued throughout the 1870s, it became clear to the U.S. government that the Indian tribes depended on the bison for their survival. As part of the government's plan to defeat the Indians, orders were given to destroy the bison herds. Thereafter, bison were slaughtered wherever they were found. Bison herds that had numbered in the millions just twenty years earlier were reduced to small groups of a few dozen here and

The U.S. government destroyed bison herds to cut off the food supply to Native Americans who rejected the idea of living on reservations.

there by 1890. Photographs of the period show the vast plains covered with the bones of dead bison, and stacks of bison skulls piled higher than a three-story building. The bones were ground up and used in the sugar-refining process, or made into fertilizer. The makers of fine bone china bought the very best bison bones to make plates, cups, and saucers. Bison horns were also used in making everyday items such as buttons, combs, and knife handles.

Once the vast herds of bison were wiped out, and the Indians' food supply gone, the remaining free Indian tribes were easily defeated and forced onto reservations.

The Last Survivors

By the end of the nineteenth century, only six hundred bison were known to survive in the United States. A few people recognized that the species would become extinct if action were not taken immediately. It was a faint hope, but these people believed that the species could still be saved.

chapter 3

A Slow Recovery

The task of saving bison from extinction seemed almost hopeless, but a few of the animals were protected in their natural habitat, and a few more were living safely in zoos and on private ranches. From this handful of animals, the federal government, state agencies, and private organizations helped the species make a long, slow recovery.

Yellowstone National Park

In 1872 President Ulysses S. Grant signed a bill creating the world's first national park—Yellowstone. One of the most important goals of Yellowstone Park was to protect the animals, such as bison, living within the park. Unfortunately, for several years after the park opened, bison in the park continued to be killed by **poachers**. Finally, in 1886 the U.S. Army was called in to protect Yellowstone's animals.

Of the three hundred to four hundred bison that had been in Yellowstone Park when it opened, only twenty survived by 1902. In that year Congress paid $15,000 to buy twenty-one bison from private ranchers. These bison were taken to Yellowstone and the herd gradually began to increase in numbers. The federal government had taken the first small step in bringing bison back from the brink of extinction, but it would take the efforts of determined individuals such as William T. Hornaday before bison were truly safe.

William T. Hornaday

In 1886 William T. Hornaday, head **taxidermist** for the National Museum in Washington, D.C., traveled to Mon-

A bison grazes beside a bison carcass in Yellowstone National Park.

tana to find bison that he could kill, stuff, and use for a display. However, he was alarmed to discover that very few bison were left in the wild. Thereafter, he worked tirelessly to persuade others that the remaining bison needed to be preserved.

A close view reveals the rough texture of a bison's horn.

Ten years later the New York Zoological Park (Bronx Zoo) hired Hornaday to be its first director. He included a herd of bison as part of the zoo's animal collection.

In 1905 Hornaday persuaded Congress to establish a bison preserve in Oklahoma. He offered to donate bison from the zoo for the preserve if the federal government would build a fence around the property. Later that same year Hornaday, and thirteen other people who shared his interest in preserving bison, met at the Bronx Zoo and founded the American Bison Society. The group elected Hornaday as its president and President Theodore Roosevelt became the society's honorary president.

At that time, only two herds of bison were under federal control—the Yellowstone herd and a few bison held at the National Zoo in Washington, D.C. When the government enclosed eight thousand acres of land in the Wichita Forest and Game Reserve (Wichita Mountains Wildlife Refuge) in Oklahoma, the Bronx Zoo supplied fifteen bison for the project.

On a cool October morning in 1907, the carefully chosen bison were loaded onto railroad freight cars for their long journey. As the train slowly made its way through New York City, people stopped what they were doing to watch the bison pass by. In each town where the train stopped, crowds of people gathered to see animals that few of them had ever seen before. When the bison reached their destination in Oklahoma, a small group of Comanche were there to celebrate the bison homecoming. Another important step in the restoration of the bison had been taken.

Bison Reserves

In 1908 the American Bison Society asked Congress to create a second reserve in western Montana. Congress agreed only if the society would supply bison for the reserve. After the society raised $10,000 through public donations (most of which were small donations from individuals), thirty-four bison were purchased from private owners and six more were donated. In 1909 the National Bison Range began operations, and the number of bison owned by the federal government increased to 158.

The National Bison Range was established to preserve and protect the North American bison.

Over the next several years the American Bison Society worked with the federal government to establish several more preserves for bison. Additional preserves were created in Nebraska, North Dakota, and South Dakota. Unfortunately, not all the efforts to set up protected areas for bison proved successful. The society's last attempt to establish a public bison herd at Pisgah National Forest and Game Preserve in western North Carolina was unsuccessful. After a small herd was placed at Pisgah in 1919, the bison managed to survive for a few years, but the herd eventually died out and was not replaced.

Despite these setbacks, the American Bison Society realized its ultimate aim of seeing bison saved from extinction. By 1934, when the American Bison Society ceased to operate as a conservation organization, there were a total of nine government herds numbering 2,435 bison. Throughout the United States, at that time, there were 4,404 bison in government and private herds.

Raising Bison Privately

Private individuals also played key roles in saving bison from extinction. In 1873 Walking Coyote, a Pend d' Oreille Indian, rescued eight orphaned bison calves. He raised the bison with great care, and by 1884 his small herd had grown to thirteen animals. Walking Coyote then sold his herd to Michael Pablo and Charles Allard. Through the years those animals multiplied until they became the largest herd in North America. When Charles Allard died in 1896, the herd had grown to three hundred bison. The herd was divided between Allard's widow and Michael Pablo. Pablo's herd grew to more than six hundred by 1906. He then sold his herd to the Canadian government, and the herd formed the basis for the Canadian bison population, which grew to more than seventeen thousand by 1934, and now numbers more than one hundred thousand.

A mother and her calf swim across a river in Yellowstone National Park.

Mrs. Allard's share of the bison was sold to Charles Conrad of Montana. Some of those animals were part of the first bison herd at the National Bison Range, and some others were added to the Yellowstone herd.

Working for Bison Conservation

Once the American Bison Society ceased to operate, the U.S. government continued efforts to increase bison numbers throughout the twentieth century. Bison herds were established at a number of national parks, federal wildlife refuges, and national forests.

Early in the twentieth century a number of states joined with the federal government and private organizations to establish bison herds on state lands. Blue Mounds State Park in the state of Minnesota, for example, began a bison herd in 1916 with three bison from Fort Niobrara National Reserve. The state of Arizona bought a private herd of bison in 1927 and maintained that herd at the House Rock Ranch throughout the remainder of the twentieth century. The state of Alaska has maintained a herd of bison on state lands since 1928. Several other states currently maintain bison herds, including Kansas, Missouri, Nebraska, South Dakota, Utah, and Wyoming.

Private conservation organizations have played a key role in the restoration of bison. The National Wildlife Federation (NWF), for example, has taken legal action to ensure that bison are given protection even if they wander outside

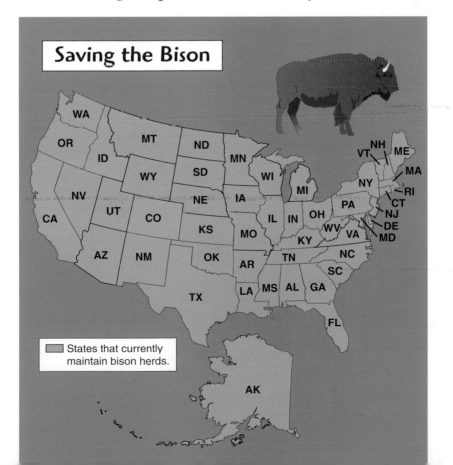

Saving the Bison

☐ States that currently maintain bison herds.

park boundaries. NWF is also working to restore America's grasslands and is working in partnership with Native American tribes to preserve their culture by returning bison to their prairie homeland.

The Nature Conservancy is another private conservation organization helping to restore bison to their native lands. The Nature Conservancy operates six wildlife preserves in the United States that include bison herds. These preserves hold more than three thousand bison on more than eighty thousand acres of grasslands.

Painstaking Progress

Since the beginning of the twentieth century, bison numbers have slowly increased each year. Private individuals, conservation organizations, and government agencies have all played a role in bringing bison back. By 2002 more than 350,000 bison lived in America. While still well below the numbers that once roamed the Great Plains, the species is no longer in danger of disappearing.

chapter 4

A Hopeful Future

The huge creatures quietly chewing the frozen tufts of grass were almost hidden by the snow swirling across the fields. In the heavy snow, even the large male bison were just a blur. But it was still an impressive sight as more than 350 bison stood eating, or slowly walked from one pasture to another. It easily could have been January 1860, and these bison could have been part of the huge herds that covered the Great Plains.

Instead, it was 2002, and this bison herd was located at the Wild Winds National Buffalo Preserve in Fremont, Indiana. General Manager Misty Smith explained how the founder of the preserve, Dr. John Trippy, became fascinated with bison when he was a child. He dreamed of one day owning a piece of land on which he could raise bison and help to restore the species.

Dr. Trippy, like many other private bison ranchers, understands the importance of bison to the cultural traditions of Native Americans. Indians, therefore, have traveled to Wild Winds from other parts of the country to give their blessing to this herd of bison. Other visitors also come here to learn about the special relationship between the "buffalo nation" and Native Americans.

Serious Concerns

Even though North American bison have made a strong comeback since 1900, they still face threats that could cause their populations to drop once again.

One potential danger to bison is the threat posed by diseases. Bison are related to cattle and can become

The bison's thick coat helps it survive harsh winters on the plains.

infected with many of the same diseases, such as **anthrax**, **brucellosis**, and **tuberculosis**. Bison, however, have the ability to fight such diseases. If a bison becomes ill, it usually recovers and does not become infected with the same disease again. Although bison have never been known to transmit brucellosis to cattle, that concern has caused bison to be killed.

The Yellowstone bison herd survived a brucellosis outbreak in 1917 and has remained healthy since that time. The free-roaming bison herds in Yellowstone, however, sometimes leave the boundaries of the park when food becomes scarce. Cattle ranchers near Yellowstone are fearful that the Yellowstone bison might come in contact with their cattle and cause a brucellosis outbreak. Such an outbreak could wipe out the cattle herds. To keep ranchers from taking matters into their own hands, Montana state livestock officers have sometimes shot the bison.

Cattle ranchers in Wyoming work hard to keep their livestock separated from bison.

During the bitterly cold winter of 1996–1997, more than one thousand Yellowstone bison were shot when the bison wandered off park property. Consequently, the population of Yellowstone bison declined from thirty-six hundred to seventeen hundred (it is now approaching three thousand again). NWF (National Wildlife Federation) is trying to help state and federal agencies to find ways of dealing with this problem without killing the bison.

Because bison need large areas to roam, their numbers could decline if their grassland habitat is destroyed. As human populations continue to increase, more bison habitat is lost each year.

Native American Efforts

Many Native Americans are seeking to return to their traditional ways by restoring bison herds. In 1990 nineteen Indian tribes joined together to form the InterTribal Bison Cooperative (ITBC). The goal of ITBC is to improve the cultural, spiritual, ecological, and economic status of member tribes. To reach those aims, ITBC offers training and education programs that help members become self-sufficient. One important ITBC program helps send extra bison from national parks to tribal lands to increase the number of bison held by Native Americans.

Native Americans are very concerned about the health problems suffered by many tribal members due to poor eating habits. **Diabetes**, for example, is a serious problem for Native Americans. One out of every three Indians living on reservations has diabetes. That is the highest level of diabetes anywhere on Earth.

Before Indians were forced onto reservations, diabetes was almost unknown in Native American communities. Tribal leaders, therefore, are recommending a return to foods such as bison meat, which is rich in protein, and lower in **cholesterol** and calories than red meat from other animals.

To encourage the use of bison, seven tribal colleges have formed the Northern Plains Bison Education Network. The network represents almost one-fourth of the thirty-one accredited tribal colleges. Its mission is to give Indians the education and cultural understanding they need to restore bison to an important role in Native American life. Schools in the network teach courses in Tatanka Management. *Tatanka* is the Lakota Nation word for bison. The course gives Indian students an understanding of how to raise bison to make a living.

In 1999 forty Native Americans walked more than five hundred miles from the Black Hills in South Dakota to the entrance to Yellowstone National Park. The "Walk for the Buffalo Nation" was a plea for the restoration of bison to their prairie environment, and to stop the killing

A herd of bison wanders freely through Custer State Park in South Dakota.

of Yellowstone's bison. To Native Americans the "Buffalo Nation" is the entire prairie ecosystem of plants and animals that depend on the bison.

The Bison Industry

During the nineteenth century a small number of ranchers took bison from the wild and attempted to raise them as **domestic** animals. They found that bison were more difficult to deal with than cattle, but they need much less human attention than cattle to thrive and multiply.

Throughout the twentieth century the number of private bison herds grew steadily. As the nutritional value of bison meat became understood, more private bison ranchers have appeared on the scene.

Ranchers at a meat company burn the horns off this bison so that it will not hurt any of the other animals.

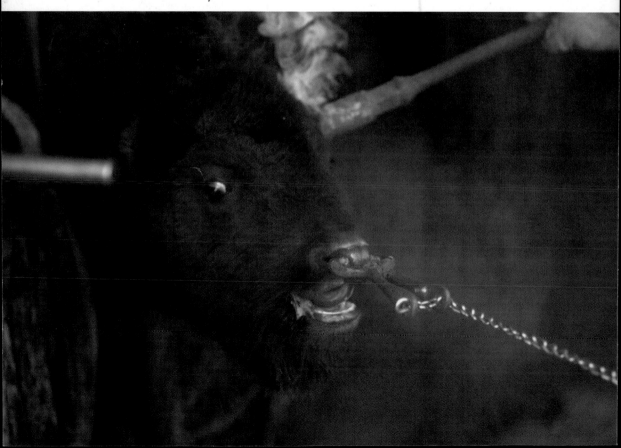

Two bison butt heads in an attempt to establish dominance in the herd.

By 1972 approximately thirty thousand bison lived on private ranches. That number increased to ninety-eight thousand by 1989, and skyrocketed to more than 2 million by 1996. By the year 2000, private individuals owned nine out of every ten bison in America. Raising bison in the United States is now a $500 million a year industry.

In 1967 the first organization for bison ranchers, the National Buffalo Association, was formed. A few years later, in 1975, another group of bison owners formed a separate organization—the American Buffalo Association. The two organizations merged in 1995 to form the **National Bison Association** (NBA). The NBA has more than twenty-four hundred members in fifty states and sixteen countries. The NBA is dedicated to preserving bison and educating its members and the general public about the benefits of bison meat as a healthy type of food.

People Helping Bison

Organizations such as ITBC and NWF are helping children understand bison and the need to preserve them. Both organizations send "buffalo boxes," with a variety of bison items, to educators to help children learn about bison and the role they play in Native American cultures. ITBC also

Children visit a bison farm to learn how they can help preserve these great creatures.

produces a coloring book, *Gifts of the Buffalo Nation* which helps children learn about the special relationship between bison and Native Americans.

Hope for the Future

North American bison are no longer disappearing. With more than 350,000 bison once again living in North America, the species is moving in the right direction. But bison still face many challenges in their struggle to survive. The dream of Native Americans, of once again seeing large herds of free-roaming bison on the prairies of North America, rests with the people of the United States.

American Bison Society: An organization formed in 1905 to preserve bison in the United States.

anthrax: Infectious disease found in cattle, sheep, and other mammals.

brucellosis: Infectious disease found in cattle and bison that causes cows to abort their unborn offspring.

cholesterol: Fatty substance found in the blood causing high blood pressure, strokes, and heart attacks.

diabetes: Illness in which the body fails to produce insulin (the substance that allows the body to utilize sugars).

domestic: Living near or to be used by humans.

grazing: Feeding on grass.

National Bison Association: An organization for private individuals who own bison.

poachers: People who take game or endangered animals illegally.

prairie: Large area of relatively flat land with much grass and few trees.

reservation: Public land set aside for some special use.

taxidermist: Person who prepares, stuffs, and mounts the skins of animals in lifelike form.

tuberculosis: Disease caused by a germ that destroys tissue in the victim's lungs.

Books

Ruth Berman, *American Bison*. Minneapolis: Carolrhoda Books, 1992. Explains the life cycle of the bison, and the history of its disappearance across America.

Ken Robbins, *Thunder on the Plains: The Story of the American Buffalo*. New York: Atheneum Books For Young Readers, 2001. The history of the North American bison and how the species was nearly hunted to extinction.

Diane Swanson, *Buffalo Sunrise: The Story of a North American Giant*. San Francisco: Sierra Club Books for Children, 1996. Physical characteristics and history of the North American giant.

Neil Waldman, *They Came from the Bronx*. Honesdale, PA: Boyds Mills Press, 2001. Traces the historic movement of the first bison brought back to the wild from a captive herd at the Bronx Zoo early in the twentieth century.

Periodicals

Carolyn Duckworth, "More Buffalo Bits," *Ranger Rick*, July 1998. Interesting "fun facts" about bison.

Time for Kids, "A Long Walk to Protect Bison: Native Americans Protest Killings," March 12, 1999. Story of Native Americans walking more than five hundred miles to focus attention on the killing of Yellowstone bison by state wildlife agencies to protect cattle from diseases.

Organizations to Contact

InterTribal Bison Cooperative (ITBC)
1560 Concourse Drive
Rapid City, SD 57703
(605) 394-9730
www.intertribalbison.org

Native American organization dedicated to restoring the cultural heritage of Indians through the restoration of bison to their natural habitat.

National Wildlife Federation (NWF)
11100 Wildlife Center Drive
Reston, VA 20190-5362
(703) 438-6000
www.nwf.org

This organization plays a major role in the preservation of wildlife around the world through educational activities and direct conservation programs.

Websites

eNature.com (www.enature.com). This site provides basic information about the loss of North American bison, and efforts by Native Americans and others to bring the species back.

Nature—American Buffalo: Spirit of a Nation (www.wnet.org). This site provides basic information about the historical relationship between bison and Native Americans, the slaughter of millions of bison by white hunters, and the restoration of bison.

Video

American Buffalo: Spirit of a Nation, PBS—Nature Series, 1998. Looks at the historical relationship between Native Americans of the Great Plains and the bison, and follows the historical developments that caused the bison to disappear.

Index

45

Dr. John E. Becker writes books and magazine articles about nature and wild animals for children. He graduated from Ohio State University in the field of education. He has been an elementary school teacher, college professor, zoo administrator, and has worked in the field of wildlife conservation with the International Society for Endangered Cats. He currently lives in Delaware, Ohio, and teaches writing at the Thurber Writing Academy. He also enjoys visiting schools and sharing his love of writing with kids. In his spare time, Dr. Becker likes to read, hike in the woods, ice skate, and play tennis.